The Process of
Being HAPPY

Brennyn Molloy and John J. Wood

Balboa Press books may be ordered through booksellers or by contacting:

Balboa Press
A Division of Hay House
1663 Liberty Drive
Bloomington, IN 47403
www.balboapress.com
1 (877) 407-4847

Because of the dynamic nature of the Internet, any web addresses or links contained in
this book may have changed since publication and may no longer be valid. The views
expressed in this work are solely those of the author and do not necessarily reflect the views
of the publisher, and the publisher hereby disclaims any responsibility for them.

Any people depicted in stock imagery provided by Getty Images are models,
and such images are being used for illustrative purposes only.
Certain stock imagery © Getty Images.

Scripture marked (KJV) is taken from the King James Version of the Bible.

Scripture quotations taken from the New American Standard Bible® (NASB),
Copyright © 1960, 1962, 1963, 1968, 1971, 1972, 1973, 1975, 1977, 1995 by
The Lockman Foundation Used by permission. www.Lockman.org

Scripture quotations marked (NIV) are taken from the Holy Bible, New International Version®,
NIV®. Copyright © 1973, 1978, 1984, 2011 by Biblica, Inc.™ Used by permission of Zondervan.
All rights reserved worldwide. www.zondervan.comThe "NIV" and "New International Version" are
trademarks registered in the United States Patent and Trademark Office by Biblica, Inc.™

ISBN: 978-1-9822-4650-1 (sc)
ISBN: 978-1-9822-4651-8 (e)

Library of Congress Control Number: 2020906980

Print information available on the last page.

Balboa Press rev. date: 06/16/2020

BALBOA.PRESS
A DIVISION OF HAY HOUSE

Contents

Dedication

This book is dedicated to you, the user, who is brave enough
to embrace change and seek help to better yourself.

We dedicate this to you and your future.

So you can live a life of truly being HAPPY each and every day.

So you may find the joys and gifts that each moment of life holds for you.

Take this happiness and these lessons of positive living forward with you
and share them as often as you can to make your world and the lives
of those you Love a better place as you embrace "Being HAPPY"

Mission

At The House of Compassionate Gratitude
our mission is to help all those who seek to live a positive,
happy life, full of peace, love, and joy.

In the role of Transitional Life Coach, we provide support, guidance, and
Love to those who are in transition or looking to live their lives with more
passion, purpose, and happiness. Through mindfulness and gratitude
activities we support those we serve in knowing themselves, identifying
their strengths, reaching their goals, living their personal mission.

Happiness is a state of being.

~

About the Authors

Years ago now, my path of personal development led me to Virginia Beach, which expanded my exploration of my soul path incredibly. Throughout my life I have had the opportunity to explore a variety of religions, spiritualities, churches and other healing services, overall following my intuition in finding a home and a way to use my gifts to make the world a more peaceful and Loving place. Focusing on the healing arts and the soul's journey, I better understand my own and how I am meant to help others. This is my path—to encourage people on their journey of awakening and soul growth. After spending the first 15 years of my professional career in customer service and sales management primarily in the banking industry, I understand how profession, career, education, and finances affect our daily living and path. Shifting my focus to the soulful and spiritual well-being of others was a personal leap of faith and also one of my most fulfilling. As a transitional coach, my work focuses on the use of my education, experience and insight to help people see, understand, and heal their relationships on the soul level. This includes relationships with partners, family, friends, work in the world, and with oneself. The goal is to see these relationships as they are now and to grow from them. With the Life Bridge Aid role and end-of-life coaching, this includes actively engaging those I work within legacy memorialization and bringing peace to the end of life transition for all those involved.

John Joseph Wood and his contributions to the development of The House of Compassionate Gratitude are immense. He was my personal coach and I am forever grateful for his friendship and guidance. John spent much of his early life as a traditional hero, serving his community as a member of the New York State Park Police and Fire Department and joining the Army and following in his parents' footsteps. Later this led him around the nation servicing our government and country in much the same way. This desire to serve has transformed him into an amazing guide and support in our spiritual work. John was born at West Point Military Academy and is a retired State

Park Police officer and 1ˢᵗ Lieutenant in the U.S. Military. After surviving a life-threatening accident 13 years ago, John rebuilt himself from the ground up. Learning to walk again, fighting pain and frustration, he found salvation in faith and inner strength. He is a Loving family man who leads his family and peers with a smile and a positive attitude. With his huge heart, he claims the humble motto "I am just earning my wings." With that in mind, he lives a selfless life under the principle belief of "duty, honor, country."

Brennyn Molloy and John J. Wood

We believe that happiness is a state of being. It is an internal experience and way of living. We believe that all lives are meant to be lived in a happy positive way. This is a choice. We believe that we all have a life path and purpose. Although lives are full of lessons we believe they are all meant to teach us and help us grow into better people and enlightened souls. In working with us and "Being HAPPY" we will strive to help you to understand how to implement positive permanent change to your mental and spiritual well being. Awareness and happiness are choices and a way of life, not labels or destinations. It is believed by some that our brains are hardwired for positive or negative thinking, that some people are naturally more positive than others. While this may seem valid some doctors are challenging that belief. There is more and more research that supports the belief that this is something we can change. If you would like further intellectual information we recommend reading "The Biology of Belief", "Molecules of Emotion", "How Emotions Are Made", "Change Your Brain Change Your Body", Breaking the Habit of Being Yourself".

Aim to keep your energy and those around you positive.

In this book, we use the words God, Creator, Spirit, and Universe interchangeably. Please use what is most comfortable for you. We believe that all things are made up of energy and all interactions have an effect on this energy. This workbook, our coaching programs, and certifications address the energy of LIVING a positive, purposeful, life and being HAPPY in this life.

In our work and this workbook, we refer to meditation and prayer. We like to remember the old adage, "Prayer is when you talk, meditation is when you listen." In prayer, you are speaking to Creator, Angels, your own soul in some form. Asking for help, guidance, instruction. In meditation, you are quiet, mindful and aware to receive this information with gratitude when it arrives with an open mind and heart.

We also recognize that not every activity will resonate or "fit" with everyone. This is normal. There is no one size fits all. We encourage you to complete each week's activity as best you can. This will encourage your positive HAPPY mindset, create HAPPY habits and help you stay committed to the process.

How to use this workbook

As you navigate this workbook there are a few things we would like you to know. This workbook was written to encompass many of the coaching techniques we use at The House of Compassionate Gratitude. Pages 7 to 11 were written to be used with a transitional coach and are optional when using this workbook on your own. If you would like to work with one of our certified coaches we are happy to refer you. Your coach will guide you in how to complete this work in line with your personal goals and timeline. If you are using "Being Happy" as a self study we encourage you to answer the questions on page 11 and 12 before you begin and again at the end of the 26 weeks for personal reflection. Then start your 26 weeks with page 13 and the "30 Day Challenge" and page 15 "Food Log, sleep journal, and exercise page" these are daily activities. Please work on it for the first 30 days. The other activities are meant to be completed one activity a week in order, the first three overlap the 30 day challenge and are meant to. Take your time, each can be gone back over or added to. Below you will find our recommended 26 week self study schedule.

Week one: ~ Goals and Happiness page 12

~ Begin 30 Day Challenge page 13
~ Food Log, sleep journal, and exercise page 15

Week two : Complete one chapter every week following week one. Each chapter is designed to take your time with, in some cases to be repeated during the week, and provoke new thoughts and habits. You may go back over chapters at any time, repeat them or add to the exercises.

The final pages of this workbook we call "Reflections" and are for your inspiration and contemplation. Please read and review them when you need an extra positive perspective or shift. They also work well when you find you are not as engaged in a weekly activity.

Coaching Contract

Intake and agreement

Name._____

Address _____

Phone _____ Email _____

Scheduled Sessions ~26 weekly sessions ~Start Date _____ End Date _____

This questionnaire that follows is designed to help us understand where you feel you are and where you would like to go over all. As well as what challenges (learning opportunities)) you may face on the way. Throughout our work together we will check in and evaluate what has changed and what has stayed the same. It is a living document and we can add to it or change it at any time. There are NO wrong answers. Our first session will consist of reviewing your responses and my understanding of them to better support you. As you work through the 26 weeks you will likely change many thoughts and there for goals.

I may take notes in each session and provide you with brief written feedback after each session. This is done to ensure understanding and help us both follow up. You are committing to completing each section of "Being HAPPY" for the full 26 week period, changing your mindset in the process. Some weekly activities may feel odd, awkward or not resonate with you. That is normal, I ask that you complete them as best you can for the overall experience.

In this agreement you agree to be honest and engaged in your own success. You agree to commit to yourself and this process for a period of _____ months.

Client signature _____ Date _____

Coach's Signature _____

All sessions, conversations, communication are confidential, except where prohibited by law or danger to life.
I am not a licensed therapist or counselor. We are not liable for your actions.

The coaching session- What to expect.

Getting the most from your session

- Clear your space, inner space and physical space.
- Plan for your session, the same time every week/month.
- Complete the weekly activity as directed to the best of your ability
- We will work together if you find a lesson challenging
- Come with your thoughts and be prepared to discuss.
- You are encouraged to take notes as well.

Why to work with a life coach.

- Helping you to know and value yourself
- Help you see and know your soul's spiritual life path
- Provide guidance in knowing the signs of the soul journey
- Encourage you to act from a place of compassion and Love
- Exploring positive and growth mindset for challenges
- Provides support as you explore negative belief framework
- Gain insight into who you are, strengths, and capabilities
- Providing encouragement and support
- Helping define goals
- Helping to identify action and next steps
- Challenging your view and perspective
- Understanding what is important /what motivates you
- Building positive and happy habits
- Examining your current habit through reflection
- Reinforcing Faith in yourself, creator, life. Faith in fate.
- Help you see your own level of awareness and enlightenment

Meet your Life Coach

Name Date _____

Address _____Phone number

The House of Compassionate Gratitude Certificate ID _____

CPR Certified _____Provider and ID Number _____

Ordained Minister _____Organization _____

Counselor or Therapist _____

EMT, Doctor, Nurse, etc. _____

Other licenses or certifications _____

Notes:

_____

_____

_____

_____

_____

_____

_____

_____

_____

_____

We are not licensed therapists or counselors.

The House of Compassionate Gratitude does NOT accept responsibility in any
way for the legal, medical or financial training of your coach.

Client Interview

Please tell us about yourself.
Use this page to tell about yourself for future reflection or for work with your coach.

Full Name _____

Address _____

Phone Number _____

Primary Contact _____ Primary Contact Phone _____

Dr. _____

Faith Leader _____ Hometown

Spouse _____	Number _____
Partner _____	Number _____
Best Friend _____	Number _____
Parents _____	Number _____
Child _____	Number _____
Child _____	Number _____
Child _____	Number _____
Child _____	Number _____
Family _____	Number _____
Family _____	Number _____
Family _____	Number _____
Family _____	Number _____
Family _____	Number _____
Family _____	Number _____

Below are some questions to help us know you better and to get a picture of your view of yourself and expectations. Please reflect on these and document in your journal. You may use a paper journal or a digital format.

When asked, please scale from 1 -10 with 1 as the lowest and 10 as the most.

1. Who makes up your household support system?
2. Are you currently seeing any type of mental health professional?
3. Have you in the past?
4. Are you currently, or have you ever taken medication related to mental health?
5. Do you currently, or have you ever used illegal drugs?
6. How often do you consume alcohol?
7. Have you ever been in an abusive relationship?
8. Tell us about your physical exercise and eating style.
9. What would you like from your coach during your sessions?
10. On a scale of 1 -10 how happy are you with your life right now?
11. What are the things that make you happy?
12. On a scale of 1-10 how motivated are you in your work/personal life?
13. What motivates you?
14. On a scale of 1 -10 how stressed do you feel right now?
15. What are your key stressors?
16. What was the happiest time of your life so far?
17. What was the worst time of your life?
18. List 5 things that you feel you are 'putting up with' right now?
19. What approaches motivate /demotivate you?
20. What have been your 3 greatest successes to date?
21. What major changes have you been faced with over the last year?
22. What is most important to you in your life and why?
23. What are the most important relationships in your life – why?
24. Is your life one of your choosing? If not, who is choosing it for you?
25. What are the biggest goals you want to achieve in your life?
26. This year? Over the next 3-5 years?
27. What are three things you expect from our work together?
28. What would you like your coach to do if you struggle with your goals?
29. How will you know when you are receiving value from the coaching process?

Goals and Happiness

The following section should be filled out in your workbook and will serve as a quick reminder of your current joys and happiness.

3 things that make you happy.

_____

_____

3 people you are happy with or make you smile

_____

_____

3 good things in a bad situation

_____

_____

_____

Goals
3 one year goals

_____

_____

3 six month goals

_____

_____

3 three-month goals

_____

_____

3 start RIGHT NOW goals

_____

_____

_____

3 things that bring you down and we need to get rid of

_____

_____

_____

30 Day Challenge

Habits and routine build the framework of our lives. We learn many habits that facilitate negativity in life. worry, procrastination. The focus of this workbook is to shift your thinking from negativity and worry into positivity and happiness. Starting today and for the next 30 days please journal 3 things you are grateful for each day. The goal is to find 3 different things each day. No repeating. This list can be reread at any time for encouragement and motivation.

1 _____

_____

_____

2 _____

_____

_____

3 _____

_____

_____

4 _____

_____

_____

5 _____

_____

_____

6 _____

_____

_____

7 _____

_____

_____

8 _____

_____

_____

9 _____

_____

_____

10 _____

_____

_____

11 _____

_____

_____

12 _____

_____

_____

13 _____

_____

_____

14 _____

_____

_____

15 _____

_____

_____

16 _____

_____

_____

17 _____

_____

18 _____

_____

19 _____

_____

20 _____

_____

21 _____

_____

22 _____

_____

23 _____

_____

24 _____

_____

25 _____

_____

26 _____

_____

27 _____

_____

28 _____

_____

29 _____

_____

30 _____

_____

Food Log, sleep journal, and exercise

Caring for your physical being is a key part of wellbeing. Managing these in a mindful healthy way is imperative to living well. It is recommended to engage in three 30 minute workouts each week to maintain general health. Eating a well balanced diet that fits your personal needs, goals and lifestyle is always paramount to being well in body, mind, and spirit. We recommend that if you find yourself tired, over or underweight take the next step in seeing a professional such as a health coach or nutritionist. Take some time this month to track your current routine. Daily documentation can give a big picture view of your habits and routines, thus allowing you the perspective to make changes and adjust. Please use a journal to journal your food and daily activity over the next 30 days, along with the other activities laid out for the next month.

_____
_____
_____
_____
_____
_____
_____
_____
_____
_____
_____
_____
_____
_____
_____
_____
_____
_____
_____
_____

Shifting to gratitude in the moment

When we are plagued with worry it can be easy to get lost in it. Especially when confronted with a challenge, unpleasant event or going to sleep. Being grateful can take many forms while in the moment. Later in this workbook on page 39 we will work more with understanding the blessing in times of madness, but for now we will work with shifting focus for positive energy.

When confronted with worry form the new habit of saying "Thank you" over and over. Start this new habit by identifying what your worry triggers are.

Is it driving? Work? Money? Health?

My worry trigger is _____

My worry trigger is _____

My worry trigger is _____

Before engaging in anything that triggers you take a deep breath through your nose and out through your mouth and repeat. "Thank you, Thank you, Thank you," over and over. Focus on the gratitude of the words and what would make the worry less. Happy people at work, $50,000 in your bank balance etc. Say the words over and over, even if and especially if they feel silly or if they do not feel true yet. Also use non focused time to repeat them such as when driving, showering, before you sleep. Commit to yourself when you will use this new grateful habit

I will repeat "Thank you, Thank you, Thank you," when I _____

I will repeat "Thank you, Thank you, Thank you," when I _____

I will repeat "Thank you, Thank you, Thank you," when I _____

I will repeat "Thank you, Thank you, Thank you," when I _____

Faith in Fate, Light at the end of the tunnel

When things are rough it is important to remember that things will get better. As you navigate life you will come across spiritual road signs. Markers if you will, that you are on the right path. When you are quiet and in prayer you can ask for help, signs, messages to support your forward movement. To receive this kind of guidance you need to know what your signs are. Sit and think about the ones you have received and appreciated in the past. These are the ones you will be most open to going forward. Write them in the space below. You can add more that you would like to receive. If you aren't sure if you have received signs or messages like this before take time to review this list or think of your own. Write them down and ask Creator and your angels to use them with you soon to show you the way. Going forward, keep experiences with these in your journal. Write down when you notice your signs and always express your gratitude. Thank those who sent them to you.

_____
_____
_____
_____
_____
_____
_____
_____
_____
_____
_____
_____
_____
_____
_____
_____
_____
_____
_____
_____

Art By Charlotte Rose Wood

Signs from the Universe

Horse Shoes Four	**License Plates**	**Birds Lady Bugs**
Leaf Clovers	**Dragon Flies**	**Shooting Stars**
Rainbows	**Repeating Numbers (1111, 444, 369)**	**Pennies or coins**
Angels	**Stars Feathers**	**Wings**
Butterflies		
Animal Signs		

_____   _____   _____

_____   _____   _____

_____   _____   _____

_____   _____   _____

_____   _____   _____

_____   _____   _____

Drive or Walk for a Sign The "Right or Left" Adventure

Getting in touch with how the Universe communicates with you can support you in dramatic ways. Reinforcing your faith and connection. In this exercise, take a walk or a drive with no destination. Be sure you set out with time to explore and see where the road takes you. Set the intention with a clear mind that the Universe sends you a clear sign that you will understand and receive. There should be no specific outcome, or sign. This is why we suggest you spend some time defining what they are for you on page13. Keep in mind that these can and often do change with time and experience. This is also known as mindfulness or active meditation.

What signs did you receive on your drive?

_____ _____

_____ _____ _____

_____ _____

_____ _____ _____

_____ _____

_____ _____ _____

Meditation

Meditation calms the mind, settles it. It can balance both sides of your brain, bringing them in sync. This is why so many overthinkers and worriers find it beneficial. This unity of thought increases concentration and productivity. While decreasing overthinking and anxiety. Take some time to practice each of these. Meditation isn't only about stillness and silence. It is about being present and mindful. Mindfulness is the process of purposely bringing one's attention to experiences occurring in the present moment. We say "being in the now." Being happy is about happiness in the present moment. Directing your attention to the current moment with joy, gratitude and happiness. We encourage mindful thought and prayer before, during or after meditation. It is often said "Prayer is when you talk to God and meditation is when you listen." This supports your personal relationship with your creator and intentional conversation.

10-15 Minutes

Meditation can be easy. To begin, take a few minutes of simple deep breathing. In through the nose out through the mouth. Just focus on the feeling of breath through your being. Start with doing this for 5 or 10 breaths and build to 50. Keeping them slow and steady. This is the beginning of meditation.

Grounding & Connecting

Meditation for grounding and connection is useful for those with anxiety, high energy and stress. For this we recommend standing, your feet bare on the earth, your hands free to reach upward if you see fit. Begin with three deep breaths in through the nose slowly out through the mouth.

Now envision roots growing out of your feet, down through the earth and wrapping around the core of our planet for strength and stability. Draw that strength back upwards through your feet and into your body. This feeling of earthly power can make you more confident and brave as it comes up and into your heart. As it reaches your throat, your voice has new courage and then your mind is clear.

Stretch your arms over your head picturing your fingers extending heavenward and out into the Universe. Brushing past clouds and stars to the infinite source of energy and wisdom. This Love and light is available for you to draw back down into yourself like a cool rain. Easing into your mind and down to your soul clearing past worries and pain. You are now full of all that Heaven has to offer.

Request for Guidance.

Today I ask for divine guidance. I accept and seek the truth in my path and ask the Universe, Creator, God to lead the way in my life. To shift me as needed. To show me where I am meant to be. To bring me peace, Love, joy and prosperity. I invite and accept the changes and intervention needed to receive this and live the life meant for me.

⌒

Release Mantra

I release back to the Universe, God, Creator any energy, feelings, thoughts, habits, beliefs or impressions that are negative, hurtful and that no longer serve my highest good. No matter where or when I attached them, even if they do not belong to me or never did. I release them with ease and peace from every part of my soul and every cell in my being.

⌒

Self Care Shower for Release

Water makes up over 60% of a human body and our planet.
Water is a powerful way to release negative energy. This release will work in the rain, a river, the ocean or even the shower. To begin, decide what water source you will be using. Clean, fresh, moving water, from a natural source is best. Pool water or publicly sourced water such as tap water will work.

Stand with your feet in the water at least ankle deep envision every cell in your body releasing darkness and negativity. These little bits flow from each organ, each pore, to the surface of your skin. The water catches them, washing them away. Down the drain, out to sea. Work from head to toe picturing this. Releasing negativity, fear, or stress.

⌒

Empowerment Prayer for Personal Knowing

Shining light to the deepest parts of myself. Awakening my inner knowing and speaking voice to my happy dreams. I ask that all I need to know to move forward is illuminated. I am gifted with the sight, knowledge and strength to be fully present and active in the changes that await me. That heaven and the stars of fate shine brightly on my path and lead me to the place that best supports my future. Any old fears or unneeded reservations, framework or outdated belief is cast off by my will and faith. I am ready, willing and able to be fully in line with my prosperous abundance and peaceful future. Engaging in my words and deeds to create my heart's desire and fulfill my destiny. Although this may be a very emotional time for me, I allow the Universe to help me take the needed steps and shift me as much as it takes. And ask for the compassion, Love, patience and acceptance to move forward without fear. I consent to my highest good. ~Full Moon Eclipse July 27th 2018

Active Mindful Activities

Active meditation or mindfulness can take many forms. Walking, running, knitting, coloring are all activities that can bring this mental state. While doing such an activity focus only on it. The beat of your feet on pavement, the stitch of your yarn, or pencil tip to page. This will balance your mind allowing clarity of thought and consciousness.

My mindful activity is _____

My mindful activity is _____

My mindful activity is _____

Use the space below or a journal to document your thoughts, feelings and experience.

_____
_____
_____
_____
_____
_____
_____
_____
_____
_____
_____
_____
_____
_____
_____
_____
_____
_____
_____
_____
_____
_____

A Peaceful Day Memory

Remembering good times of the past is one of the fastest ways to shift energy. We recapture the peace, Love and joy of moments gone by and infuse our present moment with it. Think back to a moment of your own peace. When your breath came naturally and your mind was at ease. When you have no worries in your heart.

Use the space below to write about your favorite peaceful day. Write it with gratitude, appreciating the gift of that special event. If you can't think of one, use this space to manifest one. Write about the perfect peaceful day for you.

_____

_____

_____

_____

_____

_____

_____

_____

_____

_____

_____

Stephany E Hansen

Music and Happy Sounds

Music speaks to the soul and has the ability to take us back to memories. This is true for the positive as well as the more challenging memories. When listening to music pay close attention to your mood. If the tone and feel bring you down or are fostering a grudging, resentful or hopeless feeling it is time to change the station. There is no need at this point to replay music that commiserates with negativity. That's for another book. It is imperative in engaged happy living that we pay attention to how we feel in situations and the energy of them. Music can play a huge role. Tone, lyrics, rhythm and personal memories all factor into this. If you find yourself in a negative emotional, physical or spiritual place, playing positive upbeat music will lift the energy. Play music of any format that uplifts you. On the following page you can also make your own list choosing upbeat lyrics or even personal ones tied to happy times, people or places. Some non lyrical suggestions for using sounds to elevate your thoughts and consciousness are wind chimes, the note B flat, Classical instrumental music, Nature sounds, primal chanting drumming, or flute music.

Art by Kiah Elizabeth Daniels

Happy song list

In the space provided list every song that has ever brought you joy. Titles, themes, rhymes, genre. Create a go to list of music that feeds your soul.

_____
_____
_____
_____
_____
_____
_____
_____
_____
_____
_____
_____
_____
_____
_____
_____
_____
_____
_____
_____
_____
_____
_____
_____
_____
_____
_____
_____
_____
_____

Happy Birthday Memory

As we have said, remembering happy times of the past is one of the fastest ways to shift energy. We recapture the peace, Love and joy of moments gone by and infuse our present moment with it. Everyone has a birthday and if we think about it we can go back to one that was happy and Loving. Use the space below to write about your favorite birthday. Write it with gratitude, appreciating the gift of that special event.
If you can't think of one, use this space to manifest one.
Write about the perfect birthday for you.

_____

_____

_____

_____

_____

_____

_____

_____

_____

_____

_____

_____

Color Therapy

Color is valuable. Color is energy. Color is powerful. Each color has a frequency, or energy that align with a certain purpose and intention. Brighter colors are often seen as having more energy. Thus the colors in our environment carry that intention and energy into our lives. The color of rooms, clothing etc. therefore impact our energy, intention and outlook. By being aware of the colors you are drawn to and use you can find valuable insight into your psyche. This mental and emotional place can then be shifted by adjusting the color pallet. For example if you find yourself wearing red all the time, are you feeling passionate, aggressive, powerful?

Light therapy or colorology and is still used today as a holistic or alternative treatment and is called Chromotherapy. Sir Isaac Newton discovered in 1666 when he put light through a prism how it splits into seven the seven colors of the rainbow. Light is where color comes from. As you navigate your personal spiritual journey you will likely come to know many faiths that describe the soul as light. Whether it is called God's light, light being etc. We believe this too. Thus you need balance and brightness in your colors. Be the light. Keep in mind grade school science class. White reflects all colors and light, while black absorbs all light in the color spectrum. This means that too much black in your environment can be draining and leave you feeling low energy.

Art by Madelyn Olivia Wood

We have some basic descriptions below. In the space provided write down how you feel about each.

Black: Often associated with power, boldness, professionalism

_____

White: Often associated with purity, innocence, and peacefulness.

_____

Red: Often associated with passion, power, and sexuality

_____

Blue: Often associated with productivity, calmness and serenity

_____

Green: Often associated with tranquility, good luck, and good health

_____

Yellow: Often associated with brightness, cheer and warmth .

_____

Purple: Often associated with creativity, royalty and wealth

_____

Brown: Often associated with resilience, dependability and security

_____

Orange: Often associated with excitement, enthusiasm, and warmth

_____

Pink: Often associated with love, romance, and femininity.

_____

Now take some time to try wearing these colors. See how you feel
with each. Describe in writing how you feel dressed in each.

Black_____

White_____

Red _____

Blue _____

Green _____

Yellow _____

Purple _____

Brown _____

Orange _____

Pink _____

How do your descriptions from the previous page compare to how you feel?

_____
_____
_____
_____
_____
_____
_____
_____
_____
_____

How lovely yellow is! It stands for the sun.☀ – Vincent Van Gogh

Manifesting Abundance

Print the check, then fill in the date, your name, and the amount you wish to receive. Keep your Abundance Check in a prominent position where you will see it daily, such as on your vision board. Everytime you see your Abundance Check, feel as though you've received the money, and be grateful for it. Repeat your "Thank you, Thank you, Thank you"

Bank of Universal Abundance
Prosperity and Gratitude

Date _____

CHECK # 1111

PAY TO THE ORDER OF _____ $ [   ]

IN THE AMOUNT OF _____ DOLLARS

DRAWER: THE GRATITUDE BANK OF THE UNIVERSE
              ACCOUNT OF UNLIMITED ABUNDANCE

MEMO_____   SIGNED _____

|:123 456789   [: 987 654321 000 :]   1111

NOT NEGOTIABLE

Clutter Clearing

Cluttered space is known to be a sign of a cluttered mind. Clearing space such as corners, closets, bookshelves, or cupboards are symbolic of clearing the mind. As we focus on releasing the old energy of things we no longer need or that are broken etc we release that old energy and clear space physically, mentally and emotionally.

To begin this process choose a room or project each week. We suggest starting in your bedroom, because this is where you rest your mind and body. The closet and under your bed are a great place to begin. Here is a list of suggestions to get rid of:

- Broken items
- Anything your haven't used in 12 months
- Outdated items with expiration dates (food and cosmetics)
- Dark or black clothing, they tend to enhance negative thinking
- Things that represent people no longer in your life. IE old partners. or jobs
- Paper clutter, new paper, magazines, monthly utility bills (automat your billing) cards.
- Extra or unused pots, pans, dishes, storage containers
- Electronic clutter, cords, cds, DVDs
- Clothing that is too large, too small or damaged.
- Tools, crafts, nicknacks

While clearing put on happy music, open the windows, have a lot of natural light if possible. Remember you don't need the "stuff" you can always replace things if they are needed later. Simple living is easier to manage and control your home space.

Items that still have use should be donated to a charity or offered to others to increase your good deeds, help others and build your sense of purpose. Giving fills your heart.

A good affirmation for this is
"My house is clean, I am clean, My mind is clean, My life is clean." ~ John J Wood

Manifesting Happiness

Refer to page 15 for a meditative state of mind.

Manifesting is creating what you are seeking by focusing and believing it is true. Picture exactly what you wish to create exactly as you desire. Smell it. Feel it. Believe what you are creating is yours already. Speak words that support this creation. For example "I am at CEO of my own successful business" Feel the pride inside. See yourself walking in the office door. Open your laptop and begin your new day.

What are you manifesting? _____

What does it feel like? _____

What does it taste like? _____

What does it smell like? _____

What do you hear? _____

Is there anyone with you? _____

Who? _____

What do you see? _____

Describe each detail. Feel each detail. _____

_____

_____

_____

_____

_____

_____

_____

_____

_____

_____

When you FEEL this moment, be grateful, say thank you.

Invent the perfect hour

Manifesting is a powerful tool for positivity. We need to be able to see and believe in the goals we wish to attain. Including peace and happiness. In the space below please describe your perfect hour. Make it up just as you want it to be. Creating the moment for your own joy.

What are you doing? _____

Do you want anyone with you?_____If so who? _____

Where are you? _____

What can you see? _____

What do you feel? (Happy, excited, peaceful)

What do you hear? _____

What other scenes are you using? (taste)(smell)_____

_____

_____

_____

_____

_____

_____

_____

_____

_____

_____

_____

_____

Vision Board/Book/Screen

A vision board, book or screen saver will help you visualize and manifest what you want to have or be in life. It is what you want your future to be. It is a blank canvas for you to create and envision your future. We recommend creating a new one every year, putting the old one away that may be reflected on later. As things become manifested be sure to take them off the board with satisfaction and gratitude. For some, it can also be helpful to have more than one board or use the pages in a book for different aspects of life, work, family, home, personal growth or development.

~ To create a board or book ~

Step 1 ~ Start with a blank canvas. Such as a cork board, cardboard, or blank book. You can find these easily at craft stores.

Step 2 ~ Find images of the things you are looking to manifest. Magazines are great for this. Be sure to choose a variety of topics that are likely to have what you are looking for. You could also print images from the internet or create them yourself. Some common topics are health/fitness, adventure, vacations, partners/family, home, education, travel or moving, income or money, emotions, positive and supportive words.
Step 3 ~ Cut out the images. Cut out all those that you are drawn to. Don't worry about how they fit just yet.
Step 4 ~ The last step is to attach them to your board. Do this in a way that is easy flowing and peaceful to you. Tape, glue or tacks are the easiest. You will find that you may not use all those you cut out. That is okay. You will naturally be drawn to the ones you really want the most.

To create an online vision board or screen saver establish a program that allows you to add photos. Such as Google Sides, Microsoft Paint, Apples Pages, or even Canva. All you need to do is add photos from your magazines or by downloading them for your search engine. Often this is a click and drag action. You can then save the image as your screensaver or cell phone screen. By doing this you keep your manifesting images with you all the time. This is great for manifesting professionals.

~ A few things to be mindful of. ~

Think carefully about what you are asking for. The Universe can have a very interesting way of producing what you are visualizing. You also don't want to be too specific. It is important to allow the energy to create and manifest freely. For example a picture of your dream home is great but perhaps not the house number of a home you know of. We do not suggest putting images of people you really know on your board. We are never able to affect someone else's free will or path.

I AM

"Them are fightin words!"

"I am" are powerful words. In fact they are the two most powerful words in existence when used together. In this exercise we explore the ways we use these words, misuse their power and how to redirect it into powerful word magic, capable of manifesting positive and ongoing changes in your life.

I am strong, I am powerful.

"I AM" is magic. The words you use, you invite and give power to. Think of when you hear I am sad, I am done, I am broken. Defeating words that lead to a defeated energy and giving power to staying in that negative place. With our words we ask to be allowed that energy. In this case energy is sad, broken, done. Now for the positive ones. Say out loud "I am strong, I am beautiful, I am woman/man. I AM ready." This up lifts. Feel the magnitude of their influence deep from within your chest. When you use I AM in this way, you support yourself and that energy. You invite this into yourself. Which would you rather invoke?

⌒ Reframe your "I AM" ⌒

Write 2 I AM statements that you truly use for yourself. First one that is positive and then one that is defeating.

I AM _____. Fabulous! You bet you are. Do not forget this.

I AM _____. This can't be so, if you believe it is it will continue to be. To reframe the negative I AM we must look for the good in It or lessons from it.

Example are:

I AM poor —— becomes —— I AM provided exactly what I need.
I AM slow —— becomes —— I AM methodical and intentional in all that I do.
I AM heavy —— becomes —— I AM focused on my physical health and abundance.
I AM done —— becomes —— I AM ready for new adventures and experiences.

Rewrite your second one as a positive reframe. I AM _____

I AM . . . and indeed you are. ~ Brennyn Molloy

Power of words and thoughts

Words have power. What we speak we believe and what we believe we become. It is very important to be mindful of the words we use everyday. Especially with yourself. Below we list "Power word" to incorporate into your day. Both with yourself and others. These words are most powerful when used after the phrase I AM There is also space to add your own.

smile laugh	reward	accomplished
excellent	excited	available
spectacular	fabulous	energized
awesome	wonderful	truth
triumph	clean	fortunate
bright	powerful	dynamic
intelligent	strong	courageous
secure	confidant	brave
radiant	ready	light
love	sure	happy
forward	open	joy
fortunate	balanced	enlightened
gifted	engaged	aware
blessed	focused	awake
	present	steady

_____ _____ _____

_____ _____ _____

_____ _____ _____

No more "Can't, Hope, Try or Just"

These words lend to a defeated or passive attitude in life.
They are not actionable or motivated.

Can't or can not are not truthful words. There is nothing you can not do, but there are many things you will not do if you choose not to do them. Whenever you face something you feel you can not do you are really looking at the challenges and the work needed to reach the goal. What is the truth is that if you choose to put in the work you can do anything. If you do not accomplish it, that is because you have chosen not to face the challenges or put in the work. Choosing to not do something is absolutely okay. Making choices that support you in life is taking control of your life. Owning the responsibility for what you want or want to do is something only you can do.

Hope is uncertain and doubtful and second thought. Many times it has a base in fear or insecurity.

For example: I hope I will get this new job. I hope I will get a raise. Can you feel how it holds little conviction, intention or responsibility?

Faith is sure and decided. It leaves room for a greater good with determination and commitment.

For example: I have faith I will get this new job. I have faith that I will get a raise. In this way can you feel the conviction and certainty.

Definitions:

hope:
noun: **hope**; plural noun: **hopes**

1.   1. A feeling of expectation and desire for a certain thing to happen.

faith:
noun: **faith**

1.   1. Complete trust or confidence in someone or something.

—

Try is another word that is not true. We all learn everything. We start out learning how to roll over and walk and to speak. As we grow we are meant to keep learning. It takes practice and commitment to any given goal to be successful or do well. We will have things we do not naturally do "well" but we still do them. We do not merely try. We do.

For example:

We say " I am going to TRY to ride this bike" This begins by sounding and feeling defeated. As though we may not ride the bike. Giving us permission in some way to not do it. It is full of doubt.

We say " I am going to ride this bike" we do it. We may not do it well or fast. We may even fall down. But we DO ride the bike. And if we keep doing it we will get better at riding the bike. This leads to success.

>>>>>>> There is no try, there is only do ~ Yoda, Star Wars <<<<<<<
Webster's Dictionary*

JUST is a passive adjective and adverb.

It is used before a noun or verb, Somewhat defined as "exact or precise". Framing but more often used as "signaler, barely, only, or simply" It has the effect of downplaying or diminishing the following noun or verb. I am JUST a parent. Could easily read I am only/simply/ merely a parent. It is not affirming, positive or powerful. I am a parent. Is the statement in itself.

You are not simple or merely anything. You are powerful, purposeful. You are great!

Write your "just" statements in the space provided.

I am JUST a_____   I am JUST a_____

I am JUST _____   I am JUST _____

It will JUST take _____   It will JUST take _____

It is JUST _____   It is JUST _____

You JUST will not _____   You JUST will not _____

Now rewrite them feeling conviction and power. Take ownership of the statement.

I am a_____   I am a_____

I am _____   I am _____

It will take _____   It will take _____

It is _____   It is _____

You will not _____   You will not _____

Inspirational Affirmation Mirror

In the space below to plan your "Inspirational Mirror". Use the words from page 31 to write simple statements that inspire, encourage, and heal your soul. " I AM" statements are the most powerful. It is also helpful to use this space to reprogram negative statements. Such as " I am always tired" Is rewritten " I AM full of life and energy" you can work more with " I AM " statements on page 30. By seeing these positive words on your skin and body you more easily absorb them and believe them.

Manifest with Your Words

This is a great activity for goal oriented people, career manifesting or health/wellness.

We begin by stating the goal and then defining the energy and feeling of it. Next identify the " must have" attributes. Below is an example of using this for a new job. Use the blank space to create your own.

* Remember* Never use negative language or words like "can't, don't or no".

I am professionally successful.

Goal_____ .

I have financially abundance

How does it feel to reach this? _____.

I am proud

How does it feel to have this? _____

I am peaceful

How does it feel to be in this energy? _____

Must have criteria for this achievement:

Paid clients and students in major cities across the country

1. _____

Positive media coverage and excitement

2._____

Engaged and supportive team members, board members and partners

3._____

Use this space to create your own

Goal _____.

How does it feel to reach this? _____

How does it feel to have this? _____

How does it feel to be in this energy? _____

Must have criteria for this achievement:

1. _____
2. _____
3. _____

John J Wood (age 7)

MindMap

A valuable way to gain clarity on things is to break them down. Using a mindmap can help you do this. You place the main idea in the center and use the bubbles and then the ideal influences or details in the branches. This can be done for manifesting or to dissect and release the old. For the purpose of this workbook complete a mindmap for something you are manifesting.

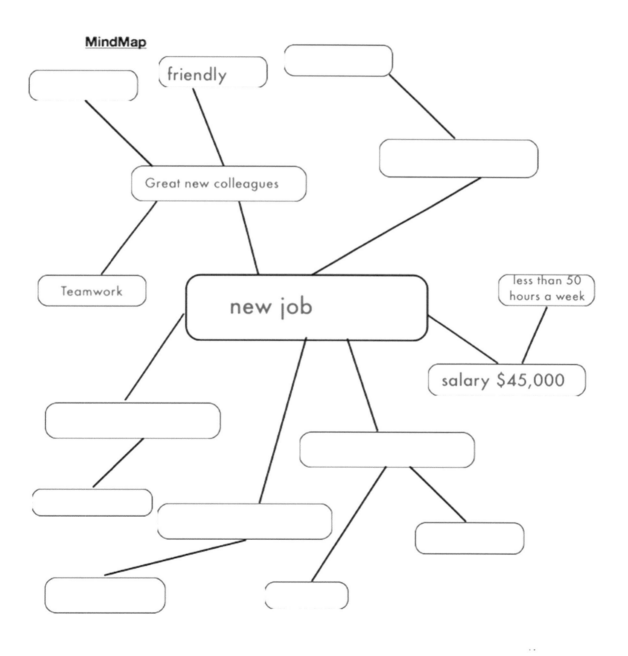

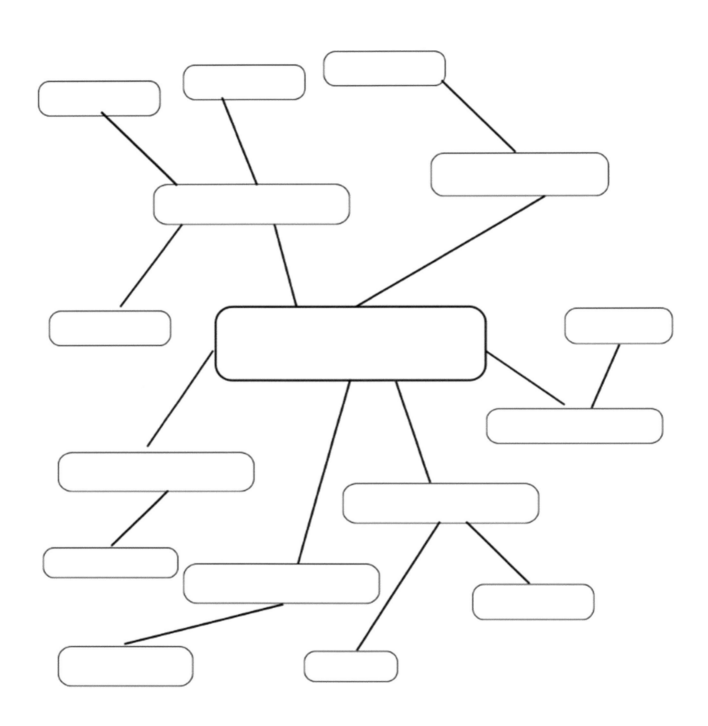

Make Someone's Moment (be kind)

When we are feeling low, down, sad, angry, a great way to lift yourself is to lift someone else up too. When we raise others up we lift our energy as well. The intention is to interact with someone else in a way that lifts their spirits, and shows them the good in the world through you. We call this being an " earth angel"

★ To find Joy sometimes you need to give Joy

★ Examples of good deeds and ways to raise the vibration.

★ Call a friend you haven't in a while

★ Tell someone what they mean to you, verbally or in writing

★ Pay if forward lunch, coffee or roadway toll,

★ Put a dollar in a random bible at your church

★ Engage the cashier or service worker in a happy greeting etc

★ Call someone you care about and ask how they are with the goal to encourage them.

★ Volunteer at a shelter, hospital or church

★ Clean up the park or near your home. Better yet invite others to help you do it.

★ Plant flowers or tree in memory of someone who has passed away

★ Donate your old items to charity

★ Mow a neighbor's lawn, or offer to help with chores for someone who can't.

★ Donate at a local blood drive, food drive etc.

★ Find a non profit to spend time supporting

Find the Blessing in the Madness

In self work and transformation we are called to change. To see our world, our life, and yourself in a new way. This is often propelled by what feels like or is chaotic, frustrating, even painful. Poverty, stress illness, death, job loss, relationship endings Each of these experiences have the potential and intention to teach us. They are hidden blessings put on the soul's path to help us grow. This takes perspective and pause. Step back from the madness long enough to dissect it. Breaking down the scenario and each nuance. When taken piece by piece we are able to see the positive aspects. Opportunity for personal advancement and to move forward.

The following scenario is an example, and space for you to work on one of your own.

Name the madness. **My job**   ✳ It is possible that you are projecting your past rejection, or insecurity on to others. This is another opportunity to grow. ✳

How do you feel about it? ___ **unappreciated**   **underpaid** ___

What emotions does it bring up in you? *That i am not good enough, or that I am not respected* ___

Who is involved? **My boss Jill** ___

In these solutions you look for where you hurt and seek to grow. Ether you DO need more training or you need to talk out why you feel that way.

Can you change it, **I have tried** ___ Can you stop it? **no** ___

How are you managing it now? **I bring up my training and experiences**

How have you responded to it? **I get quiet at work when no one listens to me**

How can you change your response? **I could quit. I could ask Jill or HR if I need more training. I could tell Jill or HR how i feel in a respectful way**

Name the madness. _____

How do you feel about it? _____

_____

What emotions does it bring up in you? _____

_____

Who is involved? _____

_____

Can you change it, _____ Can you stop it? _____

How are you managing it now? _____

How have you responded to it? _____

How can you change your response? _____

No more "Why me" asking "What's Next"

One of the most destructive things we can do to yourself is asking "why me" or the like. As if we have no control or say in life. It questions the foundation of our ability to be in control of our own life path. It paints you as a victim and allows you to believe that you have no free will or ability to improve. Merely to be beaten by circumstances. Often "why me" is thought or said when we feel hopeless or helpless. The answer to "why me" is because you need it for some reason. Truthfully you are where you are in such a circumstance because for some reason you needed it to learn, grow, or let go. You may not know why yet and that's ok. When life has you in a place of not knowing where to turn or what to do next, it is the perfect time to ask "what next". This question opens up the energy up to giving you clarity and options. It tells the Universe that you are ready to move ahead, to learn, to grow and even to make new choices.

Below document some "why me" scenarios. Ask the Creator for guidance in " what next". Use your prayer or meditation time to request this guidance. Stay open to receiving insight and opportunity. You may experience insights within yourself or from outside sources. Such as meeting people with the answers you need, new work or education opportunities, dreams of how to move forward, old energies (people, places, mental framework, jobs) leaving.

Example,

I lost my job. Why me? Response I met a friend for lunch that my job has kept me too busy to see. I learned that a company with better insurance is hiring. I wouldn't have known this if we hadn't had lunch. I had been too busy to see how much my friends were there for me.

Why me? _____ What's next _____
_____
_____

Why me? _____ What's next _____
_____
_____

Why me? _____ What's next _____
_____
_____

Rays of Inspiration

What do you Love? Why do you Love it? An imperative piece of positive happy living is expanding on gratitude. Meaningful affirmations focused on thankfulness lifts your mindset, mood and energy. Use the next page to express your gratitude. Below is an example of how to begin.

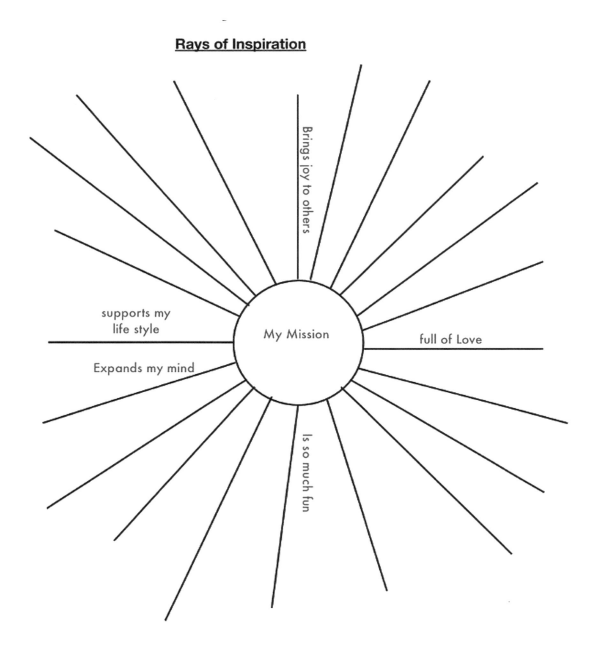

Rays of Inspirations

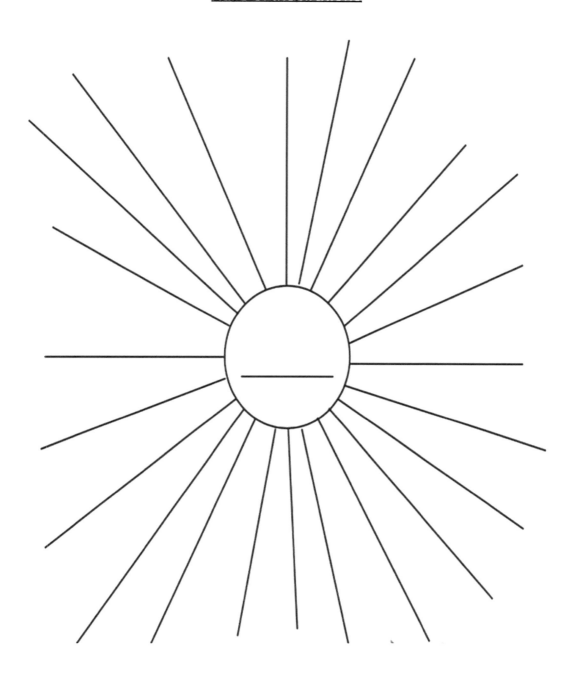

Rays of Inspirations

Learn something new

Learning new things instills us with pride, opens us to new thoughts, people and opportunities. It also is energetically forward movement. When we start a new class, book, or program we are essentially saying " teach me" " show me" " I am ready to learn." You can take on any type of new learning experience, dance, music, a class. It is also viable to work on self study. Such as a new book or documentaries on a new topic. All of these activities require the same process to learn a new idea or skill. Completing pages in this workbook are also about learning a new set of skills in positive living. Use the space below to brainstorm some ideas of things you would like to learn. Make plans to start this month Commit to creating a new you.

Learn _____
I feel _____ about learning this.
I will start by _____ on (date) _____

Learn _____
I feel _____ about learning this.
I will start by _____ on (date) _____

Learn _____
I feel _____ about learning this.
I will start by _____ on (date) _____

Learn _____
I feel _____ about learning this.
I will start by _____ on (date) _____

Reflections

Poems, Prayers, and Thoughts

The following are a collection of words, prayers, poems and concepts for inspiration, encouragement and reflection. Please add to this and make it your own. Space is provided for your thoughts on those we have included.

Writing prompts:

- How did the piece make you feel?
- Whom was the author addressing?
- What does the message mean to you?
- In what ways do you agree or disagree with the message?

My affirmation of peace, Love, and joy

As I enter the Heart of the beast
I find nothing but peace
As I walk with humanity
I find nothing but hope
As I join hands with my neighbors
I find nothing but Love

Brennyn Molloy

_____
_____
_____
_____
_____
_____
_____
_____
_____
_____
_____

"For ye are a corpuscle in the body of God; thus a co-creator with Him, in what ye think, in what ye do."

-- Edgar Cayce reading 2794-3

_____
_____
_____
_____
_____
_____
_____
_____
_____
_____

Live life as if everything is rigged in your favor. ~ Rumi

_____

_____

_____

_____

_____

_____

_____

_____

_____

_____

One positive thought today, that's all you need.
And now it will go all your way!!
John J Wood

_____

_____

_____

_____

_____

_____

_____

_____

_____

_____

"If you can't be happy now, you can't be happy." Peggy Weigle

----

Peggy Weigle

"In uncertain times faith is how to know happiness. Faith in a plan, faith in better days, faith in yourself, faith in you Creator, faith in fate. Faith allows us to believe in a brighter tomorrow and gives today peace and purpose."
~ Brennyn Molloy

_____

_____

_____

_____

_____

_____

_____

_____

By Brennyn Molloy age 10

"Happy The Man" by John Dryden

Happy the man, and happy he alone, He who can call today his own:
He who, secure within, can say, Tomorrow do thy worst, for
I have lived today. Be fair or foul or rain or shine,
The joys I have possessed, in spite of fate, are mine.
Not Heaven itself upon the past has power,
But what has been, has been, and I have had my hour.

_____

_____

_____

_____

_____

_____

_____

_____

_____

_____

_____

_____

_____

_____

_____

_____

_____

_____

_____

_____

_____

Mahatma Gandhi

"You must be the change you want to see in the world."

_____

_____

_____

_____

_____

_____

_____

_____

_____

_____

Thich Nhat Hanh

"There is no way to happiness - happiness is the way."

_____

_____

_____

_____

_____

_____

_____

_____

_____

_____

Biblical

Ecclesiastes 2:24 Nothing is better for a man than that he should eat and drink, and that his soul should enjoy good in his labor. This also, I saw, was from the hand of God.

_____
_____
_____
_____
_____
_____
_____
_____
_____
_____

*King James Bible

John 15:11 These things have I spoken to you, that My joy may remain in you, and that your joy may be full.

_____
_____
_____
_____
_____
_____
_____
_____
_____

*New American Standard Bible

Mark 5:34: "He said to her, 'Daughter, your faith has healed you. Go in peace and be freed from your suffering.

_____

_____

_____

_____

_____

_____

_____

_____

_____

_____

*New International Version

"The diseases that we civilized people labor under most are melancholy and pessimism." Vincent van Gogh

_____

_____

_____

_____

_____

_____

_____

_____

_____

_____

_____

"You are being built" Brennyn Molloy

A wave is built when the tide is drawn out from the shore into the sea.

A wave is built slowly in the receding and accumulation of power.

A wave is built in the anticipation, the awe forming from the withdrawal

A wave is built by leaving the sturdy coast for the depth of the unknown waters

A wave is built from unseen chaos beneath the surface of a calm ocean

A wave is built out the froth and foam of uncertainty mounting in the distance

A wave is built …. out of sight in what begins with retreating

A wave is built while eroding sand, and shell and shore, pulling apart the coast

A wave is built while exposing the drudgery of the briny underbelly, bits of the broken and discarded

A wave is built by the pull of the moon with a gravity of strength, returning time and again

A wave is built of unseen power, releasing with tremendous force along the surf.

Cascading the shoreline reaching distant horizons.

Changing the landscape forever with each breaking breath

You are a wave. You are being built.

_____
_____
_____
_____
_____
_____
_____
_____
_____

Today I am thankful ~ John J Wood

Today I am thankful for my enemies, for the kids who laugh
at me in school, for the kids who would beat me up in the
schoolyard, for the people who judge me who didn't
even know me, for the ones who would make rumors and lies just to
hurt me. For these people have made me stronger! Knowing who my
real friends are and appreciating the love that life is really about!
So I'm thankful for my enemies, because life is so good!!

_____

_____

_____

_____

_____

_____

_____

_____

_____

_____

_____

_____

Epilog

This is the final page, but it is NOT the end of being HAPPY. Your journey in happiness has just begun. You are ready to begin. Brush off the past and embrace your future sprinkled with everything you have learned. Crank up that great music, put on a happy smile, and wear those bright colors.

Remember if you ever feel yourself slipping back you can return to these pages for renewed insight and invigoration. Spread the joy and happiness you have created with everyone you know. Share your story and this book. Happiness is contagious, being HAPPY starts inside of you.

Truly, Brennyn Molloy & John J Wood

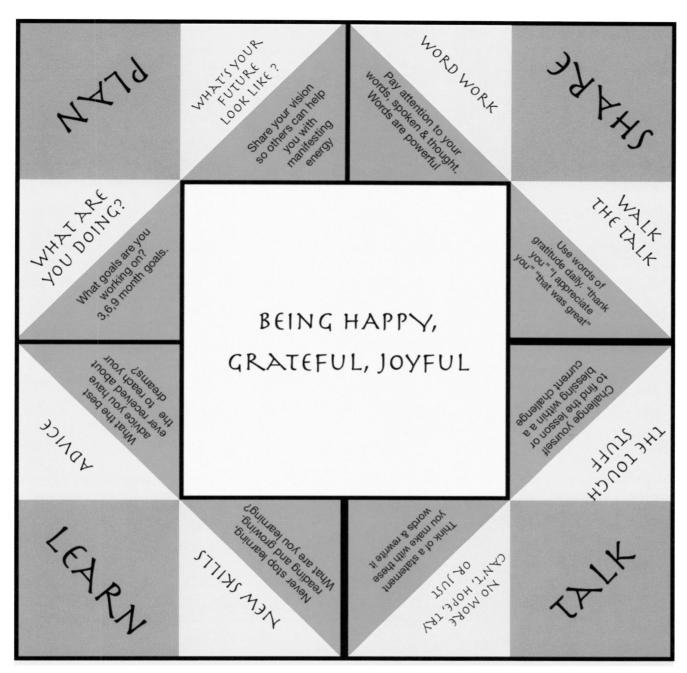

PLAN

WHAT'S YOUR FUTURE LOOK LIKE?
Share your vision so others can help you with manifesting energy

WORD WORK
Pay attention to your words, spoken & thought. Words are powerful

SHARE

WHAT ARE YOU DOING?
What goals are you working on? 3,6,9 month goals.

BEING HAPPY, GRATEFUL, JOYFUL

WALK THE TALK
Use words of gratitude daily. "thank you." "I appreciate you" "that was great"

ADVICE
What the best advice you have ever received about the to reach your dreams?

THE TOUGH STUFF
Challenge yourself to find the lesson or blessing within a current challenge

LEARN

NEW SKILLS
Never stop learning, reading and growing. What are you learning?

No MORE TRY CAN'T, HOPE, TRY or JUST
Think of a statement you make with these words & rewrite it

TALK

Cut this page out and fold for fun positive interaction.

Printed in the United States
By Bookmasters